# ★ BILL ★
# CLINTON'S
## LITTLE
## BLACK BOOK

Warning: Contains satirical material.
Do not swallow whole, or even in part.

W9-BBX-612

# ★ BILL ★ CLINTON'S LITTLE BLACK BOOK

★ ★ RICHARD SMITH
AND
RON BARRETT ★ ★

A John Boswell Associates Book

**VILLARD**

NEW YORK

A special thanks for the oral support of
Henry Beard and Sean Kelly.

Thanks to: Joanne Barracca, Carol Boswell, Patty Brown,
Brian DeFiore, Jake Klisivitch, Mike Ortiz, Daniel
Rembert, and Barbara Schubeck.

Copyright © 1998 by John Boswell Management, Inc.

All rights reserved under International and
Pan-American Copyright Conventions. Published in the
United States by Villard Books, a division of Random
House, Inc., New York, and simultaneously in Canada by
Random House of Canada Limited, Toronto.

VILLARD BOOKS is a registered trademark of
Random House, Inc.

Library of Congress Cataloging-in-Publication
data is available.

ISBN: 0-375-75241-2

Random House website address: www.randomhouse.com

Printed in the United States of America on acid-free paper
24689753
First Edition

# ★ BILL ★ CLINTON'S
## LITTLE
## BLACK BOOK

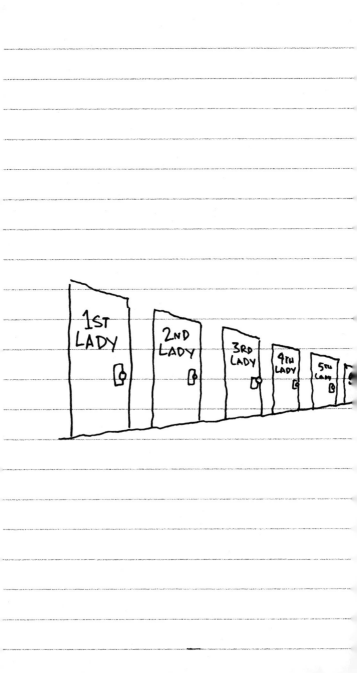

BIG EVENT! Marv A. & Ginger

My first threesome: Ginger, me
and Marv. Very kinky – really
enjoyed myself, but that boy's hair's
a fire hazard. Said next time he
gets to wear the diaper.

I'm cool with that.

REMINDER: Have FBI check Socks
for hidden recording device.

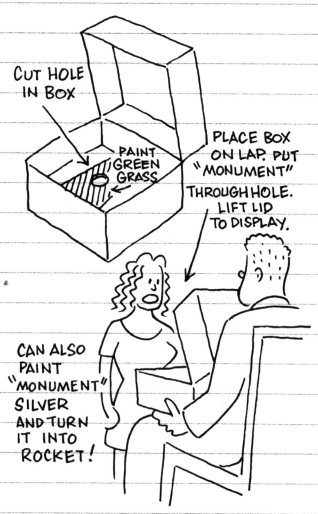

## DONNA R.

- **TELEPHONE:** No calls. Said to leave the window shade in the Oval Office half-way up when I want to see her. (This spy stuff is fun.)
- **HOW MET:** Birthday Strip-o-gram from Gary Hart.
- **COMMENTS:** Wonderful body, huge hair, does great stuff with a Q-Tip. Likes to make first move. Love the way she moans when she gets excited (emits little chirps). After 2 hours I was exhausted. Called Newt, invited him to join us but he begged off, tied up with a caucus

(Which one: Black? Women?) and swollen prostate. What a sissy.

WEIRD DREAM: Government shakeup. New Cabinet composed of Victoria's Secret models and Arianna Huffington.

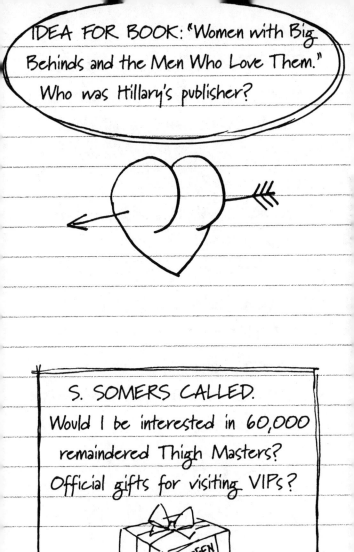

PAULA J.

- TELEPHONE: Just leave messages with "Bum" at the trailer park

- HOW MET: Can't recall. (Was she the Jehovah Witness selling the Watch Tower?)

- FAVORITE APHRODISIAC: Little Debbie Snacks.

- SWEETEST MOMENT: Asked me where babies come from.

- PET NAME: Calls me her "Southern Comfort" (I don't get it)

- SCARIEST MOMENT: Hide-a-bed suddenly closed.

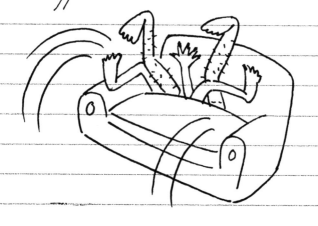

- SIGN THAT SHE'S GROWING
AROUSED: Chews her gum faster

- MOST EMBARRASSING MOMENT:
State troopers asked us to keep it
down, the neighbors were complaining
about the noise — (one lousy little
rebel yell?)

YEEE·HAH!

- COMMENTS: Seemed optimistic
about my chances for re-election.

NEW THOUGHT RE PAULA:
Have IRS audit the shit out of her

CINDY A.

- HOW MET: White House mixer.

- MOMENT SHE WAS MINE:

Gave her a White House pen

- BIGGEST TURN-ON: Gently

blowing in her ear and sniffing her

Mango Mangle body splash

- BIGGEST TURN-OFF: Got

annoyed when we did it on her

backpack. Said it crushed her Oreos.

- HIGHLIGHT OF ENCOUNTER:

Put a smile on her face, though I

was really pressed for time (had

Yassir Arafat on hold).

- COMMENTS: Funny, I don't feel

50. Cindy possible date for New

Year's Eve? Parents let her stay up

late?  Have Hillary make a call.

*LET ME KEEP HER BARBIE!*

# GENNIFER F. ("My favorite G Spot")

- Tel: 1-900 Panties (last call cost me $147.80)
- CODE NAMES: Her - "Tigress"
  Me - "Heidi"
- FAVORITE POSITION: Me on bottom, her checking for paparrazi
- BIGGEST TURN-ON: sipping champagne in G's jacuzzi, reading Jane Austen to each other.

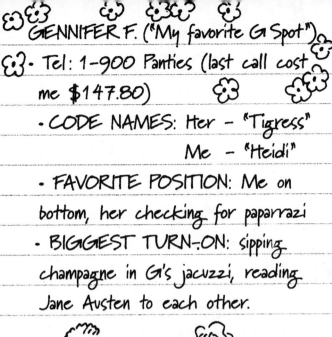

- BIGGEST TURN-OFF: First thing after sex, G. has annoying habit of fixing her make-up in the ceiling mirror.
- COMMENT: Found one of Starr's hair plugs under her bed. What gives?

# M. THATCHER.

- HOW MET: Duty-free shop, Heathrow
- FAVORITE APHRODISIAC: High tea and peanut brittle
- BIGGEST TURN-ON: Her nails breaking as she dug them into my back
- TURN-OFF: Wore rollers during sex which picked up weather reports on local BBC station

CHANCE OF LIGHT DRIZZLE

- HIGHLIGHT OF ENCOUNTER: Gave me Fergie's private number.
- PARTING GIFT: Played "Hail to the Chief" on my "kazoo"
- COMMENT: An older British babe, but remarkably firm.

REMINDER: Frank Gifford called.
Has recommendation for new flight
attendant for Air Force One.
Says I won't be disappointed.

COMMENT: Just joined Mile High
Club. (Do I get a little pin or
something?)

NEW DESIGN FOR OVAL OFFICE
(ORAL OFFICE? HA-HA)
The Barbara Bush Spanking Study
The Teddy Roosevelt Rough Rider Study
OATS
PEACE
JIMI
LOVE
The Warren G. Harding Hippie Pad Study
The Orville Faubus Study

# PICKUP LINES THAT SEEM TO WORK.

1. My wife doesn't understand me (worked on Gennifer)

2. You need the practice (worked on Hillary)

3. You strike me as a very deep person (worked on Monica)

4. I feel I already know you (worked on Susan McDougal)

5. What's your sign? (worked on Hillary's astrologer.)

6. Hi. I'm the President of the United States. Want to know what you can do for your country? (worked on Heather, Hay-Adams Bar.)

**HELLO, MY NAME IS**

*The President*

**WHAT'S YOURS?**

Today addressed United Nations.

Resisted advance made by Madeline A.

Do I have willpower or what?

Yet another intern who wants sex.

What would Kennedy have done?

# GINGER O.

- **HOW MET:** Personal ad.
- **TELEPHONE:** None. Can make only outgoing calls. (Hooter's very strict.)
- **OUTSTANDING SEXUAL ASSET:** Overbite. Her love nibbles made exit wounds.

✭✭✭✭! →

- **FAVORITE MOMENT:** Tried it in the Lotus position (me on top, lotus on bottom)
- **NICEST COMPLIMENT:** Called it her "Precious Cheeselog."
- **COMMENT:** Also wanted her toes sucked! (Carville calls it "shrimping." How does he know?)

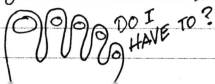

DO I HAVE TO?

HAVE OUR DEBUGGING GUYS
CHECK OVAL OFFICE.

Those little Christmas tree air
fresheners look suspicious.

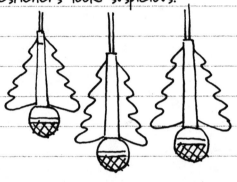

3-hour conference with K. Starr.
Debated virtues of olive oil vs. baby
oil. Which for arugula? Which for
body massage? Will let grand jury
decide.

# NOONER WITH IVANA T.

Great body, strong legs, good for pulling plow.

Her cabbage pirogies caused monster flatulence. Broke wind about a thousand times. Very embarrassed but Ivana kind – said my body noises cute, called them "little baby boomers."

Will she see me again?

(Hate that her alimony is more than my salary.)

• 35th phone call from Barbara W. Think she digs me....maybe just wants an interview. Nah.

REMINDER: Send extravagant gift to H. She gave me a standing ovation for our "romantic evening," though I had performance anxiety (that Lincoln bedroom is creepy).

NOTE: Get Spice Girls to entertain at next state dinner. Have Baby Spice and Sporty Spice sit next to me.

## SEPARATED AT BIRTH?

PAULA     BUDDY

Confrontation with Hillary over peccadillos during stay at Camp David (female guards in hiking shorts irresistible). Assured her that "It wasn't the same without you." H. pacified.

Fax from Stephanopoulos: Says it's not a good idea to give each woman I sleep with a key to the White House.

SKI TRIP TO VAIL. Tried to do it on chair lift with A's wife. Couldn't. Fear of heights. Didn't want her to think me impotent. Blamed frostbite. She didn't buy it.

Off-the-record picnic with
Swedish au pair I hired for Buddy.
Stuffed her with Chablis and Pop Tarts
but nothing doing. Said she was a
"good girl" but caved when I promised
her a green card.

Power is intoxicating.

★✩★✩★✩★✩★✩★✩★✩★✩★✩★✩★✩✩★✩★✩

## INTERNS FOR BUDDY?

JODIE G.

- HOW MET: Selling Girl Scout cookies door to door.

- WHAT DID: Just ate cookies. She still had to visit Pentagon, J. Edgar Hoover building, Capitol and IRS

- COMMENT: Told me she'd be back. Then called and said she was grounded.

Annoying call from Vernon. Says Special Prosecutor investigating improprieties re air kisses I gave to Mother Theresa.

NOONER M.

Couldn't go to my place. Big reception for Spanish? French? Dutch? Head of State? Luckily room available at Watergate and nobody recognized me! (Wore Oliver North mask.)

IT WORKED! —
DOORMAN
SALUTED ME!

• Frustrating peace trip to Israel No oral sex. Seems all women strictly kosher.   Oh, well.

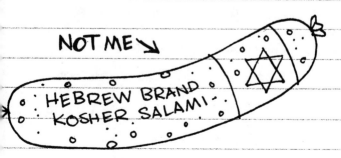

NOT ME ↘

HEBREW BRAND KOSHER SALAMI

MABLE Q:
- HOW MET: Casting call for
  interns. Can't type, can't file,
  Humongous breasts.
- WHERE WE MADE OUT:
  Oval O. — caused crisis when she
  sat on Red Alert Button. Sent
  3 carriers to the Gulf.

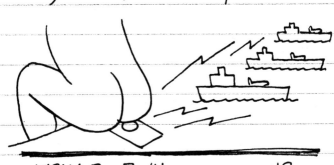

KISHA R.: Possible new conquest?
Excellent report from Vernon on his
return from Florida Spring Break.
Hold upcoming World Economic
Conference in Fort Lauderdale.

LOOK AT
THOSE NUTS!

# AGENDA FOR SECOND TERM

- End World Hunger
- Do it with Nancy Reagan
- Make world better place
- Put Gays in Space, on Supreme Court -- Everywhere
- Balance budget
- Invade Rio during Carnival with Commander-in-Chief (Yours truly) leading the charge
- Achieve real health care reform
- Send Monica to Geisha School
- Break 80 without cheating

- Good news from Immigration and Naturalization. Said there's a left-over alien. No green card but cute. About to deport her then thought of me. Where to meet?

Yours Truly a real stud! Cute nurse helped me achieve awesome climax — while giving blood!!!

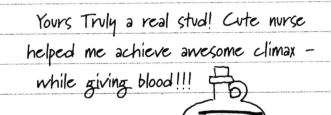

POSSIBLE JOBS FOR M. AFTER
ALL THIS BLOWS OVER
- P.R. Director, Offices of Tourism,
for Guam
- P.R. Director, V.I.P.'s Disney
World (wear Minnie Mouse suit)
- P.R. Director, top secret
underground nuclear waste depository
- P.R. Director, The Love Boat

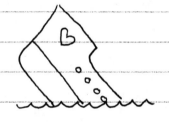

Another upsetting call from Vernon.
Says I'm being investigated for
kissing female babies during last
campaign.

GET MESSAGE TO MONICA.
If all else fails, tell Starr she wrapped
"Willy" in cigarette paper. She admits
to "smoking" but did not inhale.

## UNIFORMS FOR INTERNS?

**FRENCH DELIGHT**
Nylon and ... bare allure
Wear the ...
if you ...
top wi...
Black, ...
gree...

One ...
38...

**PARTYTIME**
What a devilish private
party stopper, all over
lace, nylon lined. Black
Red, White & Lilac.
384          $11.95

**BOW-PEEP**
The hottest little design ever
created in Satin and lace. Untie
the pretty bows and the creation
becomes excitingly revealing.
in Black, Hot Pink & Red.
385          $12.95

# PERSONAL QUALITY OF ORGASM SCALE

| Name | | Where did it | | Intensity of Climax |
|---|---|---|---|---|
| Cokie R. | – | Rose Garden | – | Earth moved |
| Barbara W. | – | South Lawn | – | Earth didn't move |
| Daisy T. | – | Lincoln Bedroom | – | Bed slats snapped |
| Golda | – | Knesset | – | Moaned in Yiddish |
| Linda P. | – | Waldorf Towers | – | Cleared sinuses |
| Gen F. | – | Bar stool | – | Hemorrhoids flared up |
| Baroness X. | – | United Nations | – | The frizzies |
| Sandra O. | – | Gap dressing room | – | Changed inseam |
| Maureen D. | – | Air Force One | – | Sonic boom |

# IDEAS FOR WHITE HOUSE GIFT SHOP

**NEAT JOKE ITEM!**
~~BUDDY'S DOG HOUSE~~
Pet Buddy!
Play with Buddy!

**LUCKY BILL COIN**
Two faced, always lands heads-up

~~BAD DOG!~~ Fake Buddy mess. Odorless.

## OFFICIAL PRESIDENTIAL BRA
### Exact replicas of Capitol dome!

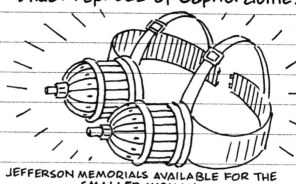

JEFFERSON MEMORIALS AVAILABLE FOR THE SMALLER WOMAN

EGO-BOOSTING WILLY RULER    ← ACTUAL SIZE

INCHES 1"    2"   3"   4"   6"  7"  9" 10

# NEW DESIGNS FOR PRESIDENTIAL SEAL

✫ ✫ ✫ ✫ ✫ ✫ ✫ ✫ ✫ ✫ ✫ ✫
BUMMER DAY: After being
jerked around by Congress, thought
phone sex might relax me. Talked
dirty for ten minutes before realizing
it was Yeltsin.

SING and SANG:

- WHO: Balinese dancers
- WHERE MET: Jakarta Opera House.
- WHERE DID IT: Presidential
  jungle hut. ←
- BIGGEST TURN-ON: Up for all
  25 chiropractor-approved "Clinton
  Variations"
- BIGGEST TURN-OFF: Got
  tangled in mosquito netting.
- MAGIC MOMENT:
  Promised me special lap dance if I
  bail out the economy.
- COMMENT: Call World Bank and
  have myself checked for hernia.

Another interruption while doing
it with M. — Nerdy aide needed
signature on Taiwan trade agreement.
AM I THE ONLY ONE
AROUND HERE WITH A PEN?

RING GONG
BEFORE
ENTERING

GUARD
LIZARD

DODY K.

- BEEPER: 917 Anchovy

- HOW MET: Midnight delivery,
  Domino's

- TURN-ON: They didn't forget
  the pepperoni.

- FOREPLAY: Pumped up her
  bike tires.

- AFTERPLAY: Gave a really big tip.

MARIA S.

- HOW MET: Personals: _The New Republic._ "Tired of Hardbody. Seek Pillsbury Doughboy Type."
- SEXUAL EXPERIENCE: Terrible! Intimidated by "Auhnald" so wore macho UPS delivery shorts. Must have gained weight. When finally got zipper closed had lost all sensation below waist.

### INTERESTING NOTE:

Revealed Arnold has strong intellectual side: Her pet name for him: "Conan the Librarian."

• Lethally dull meeting with House Budget Committee. Get through it by looking inscrutable and having Donna Shalala under the table while fantasizing about Cindy Crawford.

## NEW PENS FOR WHITE HOUSE?

SHOW GIRL BOY
BALL POINT PEN

**GIRL STRIP PEN**
(New from Denmark)
You turn the pen over and she gets undressed.
127  $1.98

**MALE STRIP PEN**
Now — equal rights for women libbers.
Male undresses.
128  $1.98

**XXX RATED VIEW PEN**

Pen really writes good

**THE ORIGINAL VIEWER PEN DISPLAYING FULL COLOR PICTURES THE WAY YOU WANT TO SEE IT.**
129  $2.98

3

# PRESS CONFERENCES –
## DON'T USE THESE PHRASES!

- boy you said a mouthful
- slip of the tongue
- pay lip service
- go down fighting
- blow hard
- go off half-cocked
- oral agreement
- let's sit on that one
- toothless measures
- trying to get ahead
- bring matters to a climax
- that's a little hard to swallow

What I was doing with Monica
when Secret Service saw me:
Performing Heimlich Maneuver, special
extreme version.   (She had just
accidentally swallowed a whole burrito.)

· Hasty fling with Tammy Faye.
Met at base of Washington
Monument. She was selling souvenir
T-shirts. Swore missionary position
would make me born again. Said I was
terrific lover. Much better than
those Promise Keeper guys.

L. BOBBITT.:

- CONTACT: Lobby pay phone, Motel 6.

- COMMENT: Couldn't recall if she was the one who cut off (Oy!) poor Marine's wingy wangy until she confessed her favorite aphrodisiac is a Slim Jim.

BACKYARD FULL OF PENISES— SAYS IT'S GOOD FOR CORN AND TOMATOES!

- SEX? Has me stumped..

# DO-GOODER IDEA!

## I COULD BE POSTER-BOY FOR PEYRONIE'S DISEASE FOUNDATION

"I am a victim of Peyronie's Disease, a crippling malady that causes curvature of the private part."
— BILL CLINTON

Please give generously and help lick this problem!

PDF PEYRONIE'S DISEASE FOUNDATION

# APPLICATION FOR INTERNS

Hi. Tell us a little about yourself:

Name ____________ Ht. ____ Wt. ____ Bra size ____

What position are you applying for?

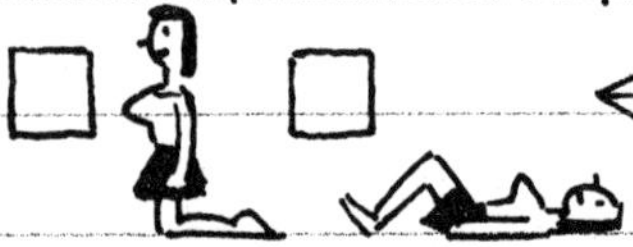

Check one or both.

## HEALTH AND HABITS

A. Choose the healthy sex act.

B. The part of the White House I work in is called "The Big Easy". How easy are you? Mark the scale.

IF YOU DIDN'T MARK "VERY VERY EASY" THROW APPLICATION IN GARBAGE NOW.

C. Prior sexual experience. Check one.

HAD RELATIONS WITH:

## THE PRESIDENCY

The President is the most powerful man in the world. Like a sultan, he has a harem of beautiful women to do his bidding.

True or False? Check one. ☐ TRUE

## CUSTOMS (Pick one)

If you met me in the hall you would . . .

## DRESS CODE (Choose one)

Appropriate attire is very important.

## SKILLS

Can you type? ☐

☐ On your knees?

President Bill

PIPPI P.

- WHERE MET: Side door, White House
- HOW MET: She was trick or treating.
- HOW SEDUCED: Gave her big bowl of candy corn and Beanie Baby.
- BIGGEST SURPRISE: Spear made her look much older.

XENA'S PLUNDER BAG

• COMMENT: Returned to bedroom. As usual, when I'm gone
longer than 5 minutes, suspicious
old Hillary sniffed me all over.
Said I reeked of M & M's and
Mars bars.

TOLD HER IT
WAS MY NEW
AFTER-SHAVE →

CK
Candy
Klein
MISTY
RAISINETS
après
shave

∿∿∿∿∿∿∿∿∿∿∿∿∿∿∿∿∿∿∿∿∿

Secret Goal: To do it on Space
Shuttle before leaving office.

I'M EXPERIENCING
RE-ENTRY!

U.S.

KATI S.

- CONTACT: None. Just quick pump, hump and dump
- WHERE MET: Texaco station. Presidential motorcade had to stop for gas. She held my nozzle.
- BONUS: Kicked in free lube job.
- WHERE DID IT: Back of station, under '83 Nissan
- SEX GOOD? Could have been better. Secret Service kept pulling on my shoes and shouting, "Let's go, Mr. President."

# ☆ WAYS TO GET HILLARY OUT
## OF THE WHITE HOUSE ☆

★ First First Lady in Space!

★ Convince Hil she deserves her
   own White House, something really
   nice out in Chevy Chase.

★ Give her Madeline Albright's job.
   She's always out of town.

★ Are they still putting people in that
   Biosphere thing?

★ Make her co-Commander-in-Chief.
   Deploy her to carrier in Gulf.

★ Appoint her Head Counselor at
   Camp David.

★ Her own cable TV talk show,
   "GIVE 'EM HILLARY", noon - 4,
   7 days a week.

★ Arrange 142 city tour for
   paperback edition of "IT TAKES
   A VILLAGE"

Call Travolta. I'll take care of the Scientology problem in Germany but he owes me dance lessons.

## LEWINSKY NIGHT FEVER!

The American people want the truth?
Fine. I'll give in. It's 7" x 2".
(Actually it's 4" x 3" x 2".)

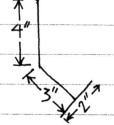

ALICE M.

- WHO: Waitress – student
- WHERE MET: Coffee shop, Martha's Vineyard. Studying feminist political theory at Smith. (What happened to Art History?)
- WHERE DID IT: Beach
- QUALITY OF SEX: Just fair. Impossible to find really comfortable sand dune.
- SAFE SEX?: Of course, made sure we wore sunscreen. (SPF 30)
- TURN-OFF: Secret Service men wearing only Speedos and shoulder holster.
- TURN-ON: Wiped away perspiration from forehead with squeegee.

## LOLA Y.

- WHERE MET: Inaugural Ball
- HOW SEDUCED: Melted when I ordered all non-essential personnel to stop dancing. (She adores power).
- WHERE DID IT:
    Upstairs bathroom
- HOW DID IT: Standing up (Hate quickies but she had to return downstairs and continue serving drinks).

- SCARIEST MOMENT: Doing the tango with pants around ankles

Aide burst in while I removed
Monica's Capezios. Needed OK on
Federal aid for El Nino disaster
in California.
ISN'T THERE SUPPOSED TO
BE A MARINE STATIONED
OUTSIDE MY DOOR?

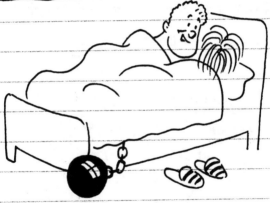

CONSCIENCE BOTHERING ME
re Whitewater and Susan McDougal.
Heard from confidante she misses me.
And I miss her.   Sex with
a woman in shackles a real turn-on.
Send cake with a file?

K. FLINN.
- CONTACT: Carrier pigeon
- WHERE DID IT: Runway (privacy no problem — airport fogged in.)
- FOREPLAY: Gave her polygraph test
- ORAL SEX: Great — kept telling me to keep my nose down. Then told me not to stand until I came to a complete stop.

I love a woman
out of
uniform!

PREPARE FOR TAKE-OFF!

~~~~~~~~~~~~~~~~~~~~~~~~~~~

Nap time with Monica interrupted by trade official. Something about tariffs, Japan, illegal dumping. Do we not have a Secretary of Commerce?

NEW INTERN causing major case of spring fever. Can't control myself. Called local Sex Addicts Hotline seeking help. Bless them — they gave me 30 new names.

MAJOR GAFFE!!!
Hillary discovered suspicious retainer on night table. From now on stay away from interns with buck teeth.

TOLD HER BUDDY SEEING ORTHODONTIST— GETTING CAPS!

# NOTES ON DELAYING ORGASM.

What's worked for me in the past.

1. Concentrate on baseball (also works for Helms)

2. In low voice repeat special mantra 10 times ("line item veto... Line item veto.....")

3. Picture Hussein in a pushup bra.

4. Wipe pigeon droppings from back of neck (During sex on White House roof)

5. Pretend it's Hillary.

☆ Social conscience acting up. ☆ Consider lending out interns to the less fortunate — Ed Meese, Marion ☆ Barry, Bob Dole, Vernon. ☆

ANITA HILL.

Tough conquest. Still very bitter.
Promised to kick Clarence off
Supreme Court and she bought it!

• WHY I DID IT WITH HER:
So hard to meet people in Washington.

• TURN-OFF: Didn't laugh when
I told her that things go better
with Coke.

• BIGGEST SURPRISE:
Intrigued by strange birthmark. Told
me it's old love bite from Marv.

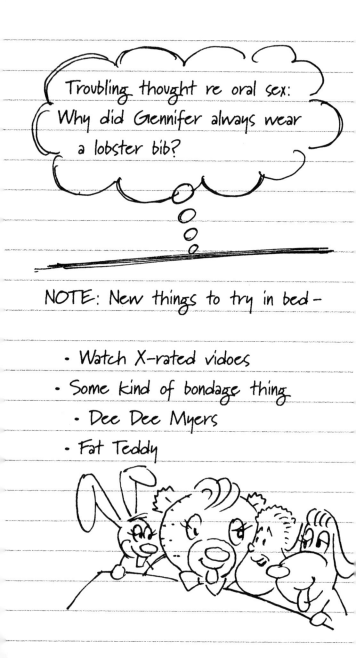

SALLY Q.

· HOW SEDUCED: Told her I loved her smile. When that didn't work, promised to make her husband ambassador to Luxembourg.

Or was it Liechtenstein?

## FUN STUFF:

PUT ON PECKERPUSS
DISGUISE—
WEAR TO NEXT
STAFF MTG.

ELLEN DE G and SIGNIFICANT
OTHER.

- CONTACT: William Morris Agency
- HOW MET: Morning jog — asked
  if I like doing laps.
- WHERE DID IT:  ABC's corpo-
rate jet. Said if I satisfied them I'd
earn bonus miles.
- PURPOSE OF SEX?

  For me : relief (stress)

  For them : relief (feminine itching)
- COMMENT: Major ego boost:
Said I was better than Jodie F.

GAVE ME
SOME OF HER
OLD TIES!

INQUIRY from Senate Ethics Committee: Is it immoral to see two lovers on same day? Attorney advised me to take Fifth but the question deserved an answer and I've got nothing to hide. Is it immoral? Yes, but with the following exceptions:

a. – One of them is your spouse.

b. – One shows up with a real appointment.

c. – It's a bona fide sexual emergency.

Just gave M. token of appreciation for faithful service (and not making me chase her around the desk): big soul kiss and book of poetry, "Leaves of Crabgrass."

# IDEAS FOR GETTING SYMPATHY

- Pressed for cash -- move out of White House into trailer park

- Have Buddy hit by car

- Hold yard sale to pay for lawyer

- Fake assassination attempt

- Start rumor I have finger cancer

- Get bad haircut

REMINDER: Buy one of those keychain pen lights. Twice I've stepped in Sock's kitty litter during midnight visit to K.

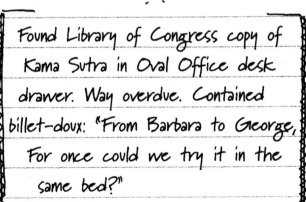

Found Library of Congress copy of Kama Sutra in Oval Office desk drawer. Way overdue. Contained billet-doux: "From Barbara to George, For once could we try it in the same bed?"

· Make note to caution G about nibbling rim of ear while I'm shaving. Face covered with toilet paper makes lousy photo op.

IS MEMORY GOING???
Called famous White House reporter by wrong name. Luckily it was a one-on-one interview.

Again had to rush sex with T. On my morning off, yet. Damn these motels with early check-out times.

Just finished watching CNBC.
Monica's mom – kind of cute.
Send her Mother's Day card?
No. Valentine's Day card – but
be noncommittal.

M. CLARK:

- FAX: 1-213-I NEED IT.

    Ramada Inn.

- WHERE MET: Post-deposition bash

- WHO INTRODUCED US:

    Al Dershowitz

- PET NAME FOR HER: "Deep Robe"

- PET NAME FOR ME: "Wishbone"

KEPT JUMPING UP, SHOUTING "I OBJECT!"

- BIGGEST SURPRISE:

Underneath cold, tough exterior is
heart of gold, and a navel ring.

- HOTTEST MOMENT: Held me close and whispered, "This, Mr. President, is what I call screwing in the first degree."

- MOST AGGRAVATING THING: Kato's living there now.

MADE ME WEAR GLOVES (TOO SMALL) AND UGLY-ASSED SHOES

- LOVELIEST PART OF ENCOUNTER: Has terrific sense of humor. Couldn't stop laughing when I kept pronouncing indictment, "in-dick-ment".

- ESCAPE ROUTE: Over back fence but bumped into Kato's AC.

## TEDIOUS SESSION WITH M.

Complained we have nothing in common. Hey! Don't we reside in practically same zip code? Didn't we once share a lottery ticket? Don't we both love sexual aids from RubberMaid???

Also – wants supper money and car service for sex after hours.

Call General Accounting.

---

BIRTHDAY GIFT from T. Kennedy: Oriental rug with Sigourney W. rolled up inside. How did he know?

---

Interrupted during tongue flicks from Monica. Prince Charles stopped by unannounced. Love the British but couldn't he just leave his card?

Dear Bill,

    Met neat guy at swap meet. Bruce wants to go steady. You won't commit. I need love. Under separate cover returning Flag of Arkansas and Fleetwood Mac tapes. Don't hate me. P.S. Hope it's still ok to use your name when seeking good table at Mickey D.'s.

                Fondly,

                  Demi

· Ego-boosting encounter with Monica L. Said we had the kind of marvelous sex that a girl tells only her best friend about.

RAVISHED BY K. during State of Union address. How did she get under the podium? Remember to send her dozen white roses, ask her to return my catheter.

LOVE SESSION with Monica
cut short by knock from Hillary.
Needed to know how many for
dinner. Remember to order sign:
"Don't come knockin' if the
trailer's rockin.'"

# SOPHIE T.

- **.HOW MET:** Obsessive Clinton groupie. Climbed in bedroom window while Hillary and I were asleep. (Forgot to reset window alarm.) Said she switched allegiance from Grateful Dead when Jerry died.

- **WHERE DID IT:** Bathtub

- **GREAT ORGASM:** Experienced acid flashback

- **COMMENT:** In morning, Hillary suspicious. Had trouble explaining red hair in sink, ring around bathtub, and hickey the size of Guam.

Good ol' Hillary. She let it slide.

BUDDY

ALMOST IN THE DOG HOUSE!

Bad case of the blahs.
Aides . . . interns . . . legislative
assistants . . . TV correspondents . . .
special envoys . . . the downstairs
maid.   Need more variety.

JELLY JAR?   FILLED DONUT?   ENCHILADA?

Just heard Monica has no intention
of "falling on her sword."
What about mine?